T0065793

Divine Leadership

A One-Hundred-Day
Devotional for the Workplace

Daneen and Michael Musolino

WESTBOW
PRESS*
A DIVISION OF THOMAS NELSON
& ZONDERVAN

WestBow Press books may be ordered through booksellers or by contacting:

WestBow Press
A Division of Thomas Nelson & Zondervan
1663 Liberty Drive
Bloomington, IN 47403
www.westbowpress.com
844-714-3454

All scripture quotations are taken from the American Standard Version. Public domain.

ISBN: 978-1-6642-9144-7 (sc)
ISBN: 978-1-6642-9146-1 (hc)
ISBN: 978-1-6642-9145-4 (e)

Library of Congress Control Number: 2023902017

Print information available on the last page.

WestBow Press rev. date: 02/10/2023

To Artie.

We did not forget. You are often in our
thoughts. Until we meet again …

To anyone feeling like they have lost all hope,
we have been there! Talk to someone. We are all
broken. Don't lose hope. You are loved, and most
of all, God truly and completely loves you.

Now therefore, our God, we thank Thee
and praise Thy Glorious name.

—1 Chronicles 29:13 (ASV)

1

Be the Manager You Want to Work For

Abraham Lincoln and Martin Luther King Jr. are just two names that probably come to mind when you think of great leaders you wanted to be like when you were growing up. Now that you are a leader, what type of boss are you? Think of those bosses you detested. Did you say you would never be like that? Learn from the great and not so great bosses you had so you can be the boss you would want to work for.

Remember them that had the rule over you, men that spake unto you the word of God; and considering the issue of their life, imitate their faith. (Hebrews 13:7 ASV)

Notes

2

No Shortchanging

You have to work with people who are at different levels and who have different capabilities. Odds are you have that go-to person in your office—the one who you can pile the workload on. That's great for you, but what about the rest of your employees? Are you shortchanging them by not assisting in their growth? Get to know their capabilities, and work with them to create a more effective team.

Moreover thou shalt provide out of all the people able men, such as fear God, men of truth, hating unjust gain; and place such over them, to be rulers of thousands, rulers of hundreds, rulers of fifties, and rulers of tens. (Exodus 18:21 ASV)

Notes

3

Walk the Talk

You may have reached the white-collar ranks, but don't be afraid to roll up your sleeves when necessary. You will not only earn the respect of your team if you can show that you are willing to work alongside them, but it is also a great way to keep informed on tasks you don't always do. Don't be afraid to get dirty once in a while.

Doing nothing through faction or through vainglory, but in lowliness of mind each counting other better than himself. (Philippians 2:3 ASV)

Notes

4

Happy Employees Equal Happy Customers

Have you ever heard that your company is in the hands of your employees? Watch out; it is likely true! Be careful to hire the right people for the right jobs. They will be a reflection of you and your company. Once you have the right employees, take the time to create an environment your employees will be happy in. It will pay off with a satisfied team taking care of your customers.

According as each hath received a gift, ministering it among yourselves, as good stewards of the manifold grace of God. (1 Peter 4:10 ASV)

Notes

5

Seek First to Understand

He said, she said; water cooler drama; the tattletale. Chances are that when it finally gets to you, the story is quite different from reality. Be cautious, hold your tongue, listen to all applicable parties, and take time to unearth all the facts. Avoid taking sides or rushing to judgment until you have gathered all the information. It will save you a headache or two, as you will have enough of those along the way.

For there is no respect of persons with God. (Romans 2:11 ASV)

Notes

6

Inspect What You Expect

Yes, it's a pain at first. Why should you have to go over what you delegated? When you assign a new task, take the time to ensure they know how you want it completed. Don't just presume. Show them. It not only ensures you are both on the same page but also makes things easier and quicker in the long run. The expectations will be precise, and accountability will be clear. It will also instill pride in your employees for a job well done.

Where no wise guidance is, the people falleth;
But in the multitude of counsellors there is safety.
(Proverbs 11:14 ASV)

Notes

7

Planning for Success

Plan your work; work your plan! Smartphones, computers, calendars, or even just plain old pen and paper—these are tools to help you plan. So whatever you choose to use, just do it. Have a plan in place for your goals, your week, and especially your day. You will get more accomplished and have less stress. Encourage your employees to do the same. A simple five-minute list each morning will help everyone be more productive, which is always a good thing!

Prepare thy work without, And make it ready for thee in the field; And afterwards build thy house. (Proverbs 24:27 ASV)

Notes

8

Communication Is Critical

Didn't you get the memo? How often do we run around in different directions, getting nothing completed? Whether it's through meetings, emails, or face-to-face, communicate to your team and ensure you understand each other. That email you sent may not seem clear to the one receiving it. That text you sent in all caps may not have been well received. That chicken-scratch note you left on the computer may not even be legible. So take a moment and use an effective form of communication that works best for the entire team.

A fool hath no delight in understanding, But only
that his heart may reveal itself. (Proverbs 18:2 ASV)

Notes

9

The Three Steps

Naturally, training is a hefty job to tackle for anyone. Great leaders are not always great trainers, so a good place to start is with these three steps: explain, show, and watch. *Explain*—clearly instruct what the task entails. *Show*—slowly and accurately conduct the task with their undivided attention. *Watch*—have them complete the task as you instructed. This may be short and sweet, or it may be time-consuming. Regardless, there will not be a question of your expectations or their understanding when you are finished.

The disciple is not above his teacher: but every one when he is perfected shall be as his teacher. (Luke 6:40 ASV)

Notes

10

Dear Future

Do you have outlandish goals that you daydream of but never put into words? Don't give up on your goals! You are more likely to succeed if you put them in writing. Whether they are realistic or a bit ambitious, they are your goals and dreams, and they have merit. Always document what you want to complete. Some you will have to share with your team, and some are just for you. Regardless, the first step is to write them down. Then you can make a plan of action and take the steps necessary to get your goals accomplished. More often, you regret what you didn't try more than what you did. Somewhere is better than nowhere.

But if we hope for that which we see not, then do we with patience wait for it. (Romans 8:25 ASV)

Notes

11

Talk to Your Team

Think of the people who make up your team. They are unique individuals who have different needs. Do you know who they are or what makes them tick? You work with them every day. Do you know their career goals? Do you know their strengths and weaknesses? Do you talk to them? Do they know you care as a leader of their team? Make time to talk to them as individuals, even a few minutes. It is vital to know your employees for the function and growth of your team, and you will be surprised what a few minutes of simple but sincere interactions can build.

The mouth of the righteous talketh of wisdom, And his tongue speaketh justice. (Psalm 37:30 ASV)

Notes

12

Follow-Through

Projects seem pretty useless if they're not completed. Follow-through is essential in just about every aspect. Following through is not just for your employees but for you as the leader. You must set the example and follow through on your tasks as well. Do what you say you are going to do, and expect the same from others around you. We have all heard the excuses "I ran out of time," "I forgot," or my personal favorite, "It's time for me to go." Your team must know that follow-through is essential and that everyone plays a part. Naturally things can arise, but you must be able to count on your employees, and they must be able to count on you.

And let us not be weary in well-doing: for in due season we shall reap, if we faint not. (Galatians 6:9 ASV)

Notes

13

Take Ownership

It might be easy for a boss to take ownership, but what about employees? Why should they want to take ownership? If you have an employee-owned company, great! What about the rest of us? You must give your employees a reason other than simple pride. Instill a desire to be part of your company. Have them realize that they are not just another number but truly make a difference. Your employees must want to take ownership, so make it more than just a job.

Arise; for the matter belongeth unto thee, and we are with thee: be of good courage, and do it. (Ezra 10:4 ASV)

Notes

14
10/80/10

You will often see that the top 10 percent of your employees will be your superstars or your go-to people who you rely on for many tasks. The majority of your employees—80 percent—will be your average associates. The bottom 10 percent will be your high-maintenance employees or the ones who often cause drama and headaches. Ironically, we are often sucked into spending most of our time and energy on the bottom 10 percent, ignoring the majority. Yes, it's important to handle and recognize all employees, but don't forget the average Joes. Imagine what we could do together if we invested our training and energy into that 80 percent, turning that top 10 percent into 90 percent.

So then, as we have opportunity, let us work that which is good toward all men, and especially toward them that are of the household of the faith. (Galatians 6:10 ASV)

Notes

15

Leave the Bags in the Trunk

If everyone brought their personal issues to work, we would probably feel like we are working in a zoo (but without the cute animals). Did you hear what happened? Guess who broke up. Can't believe they did that. It's often tempting, but let's be real: we have to keep the personal soap operas away from the workplace. It gets in the way and causes unwanted distractions, not to mention gossip and drama. Sometimes you have to play referee, but ensure your employees and you yourself keep the personal, personal.

Whoso keepeth his mouth and his tongue Keepeth his soul from troubles. (Proverbs 21:23 ASV)

Notes

16

90/10 Reaction

Once I heard this, it made me truly think twice about how to respond to situations that occur every day in the workplace. How often does something happen that doesn't go our way and we tend to act like a petulant child? Next time something happens, keep in mind that often 10 percent is what happens to us and 90 percent is how we react to it. We didn't get that promotion this time, a supply order will be delayed, we lost a big client, etc. Some things we can fix, but we often cause more problems for ourselves and others around us with how we respond to situations. Keep levelheaded, and instead of whining, get down to business and make it work.

With all lowliness and meekness, with longsuffering, forbearing one another in love. (Ephesians 4:2 ASV)

Notes

17

Teamwork

Teamwork is not a one-man show. It's about ensuring each team member knows what their job is and doing it to the best of their ability. One member does not do their job and the entire team can be affected. On the flip side, if everyone does their job well, you can have a smooth-running show. A good leader is essential to any team, and you have a job just like everyone else. A team that works together can reach amazing feats. Just take a look at history. Everyone loves a good underdog story. We see it often enough. But take a look at how they got there. It usually includes hard work, some tough learning experiences, a team that can trust in each other, and a leader who will bring them to victory.

Two are better than one, because they have a good reward for their labor. For if they fall, the one will lift up his fellow; but woe to him that is alone when he falleth, and hath not another to lift him up. Again, if two lie together, then they have warmth; but how can one be warm alone? (Ecclesiastes 4:9–11 ASV)

Notes

18

Morale

Let's just all hold hands and sing. OK, maybe it's not that easy. However, bad morale can destroy a workplace. Since there can be a multitude of reasons why your workplace is experiencing doom and gloom, it is important to find the source. Talk to your employees and see why and where it's coming from; everyone will have bad days, but that should not be every day. Are your employees bringing too much baggage to the workplace? While you're at it, make sure you're not part of the problem. Employees should not be working in fear or dread coming to work. Bad morale is very contagious, but thankfully you can find the cure.

Neither as Lording it over the charge allotted to you, but making yourselves examples to the flock. (1 Peter 5:3 ASV)

Notes

19

Look for the Good Stuff

How often do we think of an inspection or the big boss coming as something bad? The big, big boss is coming today, and we scurry around to ensure everything is in order before he or she comes. The one thing you realized you missed, he or she finds, and what is soon the focus? The other 99 percent is great (but is soon forgotten or not even recognized) and a snapshot of this perceived reality is created. As leaders, is there a habit of often only focusing on what's wrong? Or not even looking at what's right? Naturally, we have to work on correcting what needs to be improved, but we can't neglect what is going right. Only focusing on the bad and never the good can take root and destroy your morale, your team, and essentially your company.

Let no man seek his own, but each his neighbor's good. (1 Corinthians 10:24 ASV)

Notes

20

It's That Time

Having personally struggled with habitually being late, I can attest that it can be conquered and is simply making a decision to make it happen. It is important for everyone to be held accountable and should start with the leaders to set the example. Being timely is productive, professional, and a good sign of a well-organized workplace. Naturally, things occasionally arise, but that should be the exception. We can all think of that one person who always has an excuse, always is late, and is often the butt of jokes because of it. Choose not to be that person or allow it on your team. You will see a happier and less stressed environment because of it, so double-check those clocks!

Look therefore carefully how ye walk, not as unwise, but as wise; redeeming the time, because the days are evil. (Ephesians 5:15–16 ASV)

Notes

21

Count on Me

Take a moment and think of your go-to people. You would likely include dependability in their list of virtues. We have to be able to trust in our team to be there, get it done, and do it right. It must start with the leaders of the team to set the example. I hate to admit it, but there were times when I would have a backup employee ready if I had "that" employee scheduled when I had a tight timeline. An effective team does not have room for employees you can't count on. Life happens, sometimes calling out or having to leave early is a part of life, but it should not be a way of life. Have employees you can trust and depend on, and if you can't, then find out why and proceed from there. You're not being fair to the other team members to have to continually pick up the slack, and allowing it in your workplace will create strife, stress, and a negative impact all around.

Here, moreover, it is required in stewards, that a man be found faithful. (1 Corinthians 4:2 ASV)

Notes

22

Don't You Look Sharp!

What's on the outside counts too! Take a moment to look in the mirror and think of what others see (and smell). First impressions can be important in our society, and our appearance can make an impact. Just about anyone can think of a person where you inwardly questioned their personal hygiene; no one wants to have that conversation with an employee, but it is sometimes necessary. Appearance also extends to your work area and even your car. Think of outward appearances and what customers and employees see when they look at you. You are the example, so rub-a-dub-dub!

And God created man in his own image, in the image of God created he him; male and female created he them. (Genesis 1:27 ASV)

Notes

23

Go Professional

Please and *thank-you* are still the magic words. Think about your language, even slang, and the reflection on your workplace. A few curse words or calling everyone *honey* and *cutie* may not seem like a big deal, but how does it look from the outside looking in? The bawdy jokes around the water cooler may seem funny to a few but can be offensive to others. The rude and unprofessional banter may not seem like a big deal but may seem a bit tacky to your customers. It does not mean being afraid to speak, but it is vital to any company that your words, body language, and actions are perceived well upon you and your employees, who are a mirror of your company. So think before you act.

Set a watch, O Jehovah, before my mouth; Keep the door of my lips. (Psalm 141:3 ASV)

Notes

24

Think Out of the Box

This is the way we have always done it! Most people hate change, and it goes against human nature. I once heard a story about a young lady who always cut the ends off her roast and passed it on to her daughter and so on. At one point, the daughter asked why they have to cut off the ends, and the mother replied, "My mother always did it this way and that's how you are supposed to do it." That answer wasn't good enough for the young girl so she went to her grandmother and asked why. The grandmother replied, "I had to cut off the ends because my pan was too small." This is just an example of how we can get set in our ways, which can keep us stagnate in our development. It doesn't mean we have to reinvent the wheel, but we can certainly improve it. Just think if Edison, Franklin, or Ford thought that way! Never be afraid to be a visionary. The world needs them! I would still be typing this on an old typewriter instead of typing it on my iPad if Jobs thought of an apple just like everyone else.

Open thou mine eyes, that I may behold Wondrous things out of thy law. (Psalm 119:18 ASV)

Notes

25

Knowledge Is Power

While this saying has probably been worn out, it is certainly true. Any great leader has to have knowledge to lead and direct. You must learn about your competition, as well as your customers, to effectively deliver. While knowledge is power, it never stays the same. It's always changing, and there's always something new on the horizon to contend with. Keep in mind your employees have knowledge to bring to the table. You may be the leader but may not always have the most knowledge or even the best ideas. Recognize the best idea, and praise those that had it. Don't be afraid of sharing the driver seat at times. You may have to swallow your pride, but your team will respect you for it.

Pride goeth before destruction, And a haughty spirit before a fall. (Proverbs 16:18 ASV)

Notes

26

Follow the Leader

While every team needs a leader, every team must also have followers. Too many leaders and your team is quickly headed into a downward spiral. Ensure that as a leader, you are developing and assisting your team to grow into leaders, but they are still responsible to do their part. Too often we are going in different directions and not even on the same book—must less the same page. Have you ever been in a situation whereby one boss is telling you to do one thing and another is telling you something completely different? And if you ask about it, you are the one questioned! Don't put your team in that predicament. Communicate to ensure everyone knows how and what needs to be done, so you're always on the same page.

The liberal soul shall be made fat; And he that watereth shall be watered also himself. (Proverbs 11:25 ASV)

Notes

27

Diversity

Just imagine a world full of carbon copies of you or me. Yikes! Embrace your team's differences and utilize their individuality. If there is a slight language barrier or cultural difference, then increase your knowledge and learn from it. Don't treat it as an obstacle but as an opportunity to expand your team's horizon. All of us are unique and have an imprint to leave on this world, so let your light shine on!

Finally, be ye all likeminded, compassionate, loving as brethren, tenderhearted, humble minded. (1 Peter 3:8 ASV)

Notes

28

Jot It Down

Ever heard the old saying that you are more likely to do something if you write it down? It's not just an old tale; there is power in the pen. Making a list every day may seem trivial but is often done by some of the most successful people of the world. It can help you control your anxiety and keep you grounded and productive, not to mention on course for the day. And what if you don't finish your list? Don't be discouraged. Add whatever you did not complete to tomorrow's list. After all, tomorrow is another day.

The thoughts of the diligent tend only to plenteousness; But every one that is hasty hasteth only to want. (Proverbs 21:5 ASV)

Notes

29

Customers Are the Boss

We have heard it often enough, especially if you are in the retail business. Customers are right, even when they are wrong, and if you win an argument with a customer, then you probably lost that customer. It may mean occasionally eating humble pie, which is not very tasty but sometimes necessary if you want to keep your customers. Keep in mind that customers ultimately write your paycheck and you must cater to customers' demands. This does not mean doing something unethical or illegal just to make them happy. Don't sacrifice your standards for an unscrupulous customer. However, do remember that one unhappy customer will not remain just one. They will tell their family and friends and so on. Like rabbits, they tend to multiply.

But he that is greatest among you shall be your servant. (Matthew 23:11 ASV)

Notes

30

Fair Square

Everyone should be treated fairly and with equal respect, but that does not necessarily mean the same. Just as each of us is different, we are going to have different needs and different responses to management styles. You may have one employee who works great under pressure while another doesn't work well with an overflowing plate. However, we all should be treated with consistency and equality for equal work as well as an equal reprimand. You cannot have favorites in the workplace, and all your relationships must be professional and above reproach or you will lose the respect of your team.

My brethren, hold not the faith of our Lord Jesus Christ, the Lord of glory, with respect of persons. (James 2:1 ASV)

Notes

31

Gossip

If you ever played telephone when you were a kid, then you know how a story can become something completely different from reality. Don't get sucked into water cooler gossip, including who did what and who said what, even if it's about you. Just like Mom said, "If you don't have something nice to say, don't say anything at all." Something strange happens when a group of grown adults gets together and can take a simple comment and make it the next great soap opera. Make it clear to your employees that you will not tolerate gossip. The latest gossip of the day will just have to wait. And set the example by avoiding it yourself. It will help create a harmonious workplace and avoid a lot of school room drama.

A perverse man scattereth abroad strife; And a whisperer separateth chief friends. (Proverbs 16:28 ASV)

Notes

32

Make It Happen

I often heard the statement "Carpe diem" growing up, meaning "Seize the day." Honestly, as a kid, you don't think much of it, but as adults, how many times have we talked about doing something and did only that? We talk about it, analyze it, and complain about it but never actually *do* anything about it. How simpler our lives can become when we simply do what we have been talking about doing. Naturally, we may need a plan or set goals to get it accomplished, but nothing great was accomplished by *just* talking about it. So if you want something badly enough, start making it reality by simply setting it into motion and *do* it.

But be ye strong, and let not your hands be slack;
for your work shall be rewarded. (2 Chronicles
15:7 ASV)

Notes

33

Polish That Mirror

It is human nature to play the blame game. "He did it, not me!" "It wasn't my fault!" And so it goes. Sometimes we have to point that finger in the mirror and handle it. The reflection may not always be pretty (metaphorically speaking only, of course) but is necessary to see how others view us. What impression are we giving? It's OK if it is sometimes our fault. It will happen, and we have to take responsibility for our actions and sometimes for the team as well. "First rule of management is that everything is your fault" may sound like a snide quip, but it can hold some truth. So keep that pocket mirror handy, just in case.

So then each one of us shall give account of himself to God. (Romans 14:12 ASV)

Notes

34

Go, Team! Go!

Just like with kids, we want to encourage striving for that star in the sky. Aim for higher, and know we can do better and be better. When we stop growing, we can become stagnant and lose focus. However, while we can always do better, we still need some encouragement along the way. Never being satisfied along the journey can be quite discouraging and a bit depressing. Learn to enjoy others as well as your own achievements, however small. Don't forget to get those pom-poms out and become someone's cheerleader.

Depart from evil, and do good; And dwell for evermore. (Psalm 37:27 ASV)

Notes

35

Procrastination

"Maybe this one can wait until later. Maybe not. I'll do it tomorrow, or maybe when I have more time. Next week definitely, or at least by the end of the month." Sound familiar? Come on. We have all procrastinated sometime or another, but does it make it any easier in the long run? I find that I stress out even more when I put off something that I just should have gotten out of the way a long time ago. Whether you have to have a priority list or even a timer to get those annoying tasks done, find what works best for you and get it done! Getting those least favorite items out of the way will help make your day easier, keep you on schedule, and set an example for your team to do the same. Unless you can magically twitch your nose to get things done, get off your duff and do it today instead of tomorrow.

He that observeth the wind shall not sow; and he
that regardeth the clouds shall not reap. (Ecclesiastes
11:4 ASV)

Notes

36

First Impression

Remember your first date? You wanted everything just right: your hair, your outfit, and of course your breath. Your car had to be pristine, and you may have even rehearsed in the mirror. Why? Because we care and want to make a great impression. We care what they think, and the impression we make matters to us. It does not change as we grow into adults and is even more important as we enter the workforce, even if the impression is not always accurate or fair. As humans, we tend to get a first impression when we meet. Keep that first date mentality in mind when meeting people. People are looking at you. Do *you* like what they see?

Know ye not that ye are a temple of God, and that the Spirit of God dwelleth in you? (1 Corinthians 3:16 ASV)

Notes

37

An Enjoyable Workplace

While going to work on an early Monday morning may not be the highlight of your day, it should not be something you dread. Unless you won the lottery this past weekend, then you are probably planning on going to work, so make your workplace somewhere you and your team enjoy going. Keep the mood enjoyable while doing what has to be done. Consider posting team and individual achievements in the employee lounge and not just the boring stuff. Every team is different so listen to what they have to say and consider their suggestions for the workplace. Nothing is exciting about staring at four white walls, and no one said work had to be boring. And if they did, then why are we listening to them? So go get those crayons and get colorful!

Wherefore exhort one another, and build each other up, even as also ye do. (1 Thessalonians 5:11 ASV)

Notes

38

Comfort Zone

Going out of that comfort zone can be quite uncomfortable at times. Granted, we all have comforts that we like and probably even help us rejuvenate. For me, nothing beats comfy clothes, a Hallmark movie, and a cold soda. However, I can't live there, and I have to be willing to explore new territory. Going beyond our circle of what we know helps us live, learn, and grow beyond our wildest imaginations. So while it's OK to be afraid of new horizons, don't avoid climbing them just because it's unknown or not what you are used to. Nothing worth achieving is usually within arm's reach so keep on exploring, but pack those comfy clothes for the ride.

For God gave us not a spirit of fearfulness; but of power and love and discipline. (2 Timothy 1:7 ASV)

Notes

39

Bringing Others Up

While we hate to see our best employees move up or get promoted because we counted on them, we can't hold them back. It sounds selfish because it is, but I sometimes secretly wished that my best team members would never get promoted because they did such a great job. However, I would never dream of doing anything to hold them back, and nothing is quite as rewarding as seeing one of your protégés grow and achieve their goals. You are also making room for new members to make their mark. Besides, it doesn't look too shabby for you when you catch a shining star or two on your team.

But to do good and to communicate forget not: for with such sacrifices God is well pleased. (Hebrews 13:16 ASV)

Notes

40

Training

While it may sound like a cliché, *training right the first time* is a vital key for any business. Speaking from experience, it's a lot harder to go back and correct bad habits or have to retrain because it was not done right the first time. Not only is it a waste of time, but it does not look professional either. Ensure you have a patient trainer that is thorough, knows the business, and knows how you want it done. If that's not you, then make the time and effort to have someone in that role that you can count on. Accurate training will save you a lot of headaches; I have the empty bottles of ibuprofen as proof of trying to rush through training!

Better is the end of a thing than the beginning thereof; and the patient in spirit is better than the proud in spirit. (Ecclesiastes 7:8 ASV)

Notes

41

Body Language

Remember Ariel in *The Little Mermaid?* She was able to land her true love with little more than body language, so never underestimate how your actions can come across to those around you. Your mouth may be saying one thing, but if your body is saying another, it is sending a mixed message to the receiver. Sometimes it's just plain tough such as if we are sick, and maybe those are the days you need to sit it out. Simply put, watch how your actions, walking, and gestures appear to those around you. Just as mothers always had us practice walking with a book on our head to stop our slouching, keep your body language in check to avoid saying the wrong thing.

Or know ye not that your body is a temple of the Holy Spirit which is in you, which ye have from God? and ye are not your own. (1 Corinthians 6:19 ASV)

Notes

42

Open Door

The principal's office is not just reserved for scoldings. Let your employees feel comfortable enough with you that they can come and talk to you as needed, but only if you can support that statement. Be willing to support an open-door workplace, which may not always be convenient for you, but this gives a setting for a positive environment. If your employees want to talk with you, then ensure you follow through, even if you have to set it up for a later time. Sometimes just knowing that your door is always open and they can talk to you can go a long way in laying the groundwork for a solid foundation.

Not looking each of you to his own things, but each of you also to the things of others. (Philippians 2:4 ASV)

Notes

43

Lead by Example

"Do as I say and not as I do." It doesn't work on kids so we can't pretend it will work on our peers either. Being above reproach in the workplace doesn't mean being perfect, but it does mean that you are setting the example for what is acceptable. It certainly may not always be fun, but setting and leading by example will earn you the respect and even admiration of your employees. Not to mention if you can set the correct example, then the accountability and the standards are clear, consistent, and precise. Whether you like it or not, as the leader you are on a stage, do you like what your audience is watching?

The things which ye both learned and received and heard and saw in me, these things do: and the God of peace shall be with you. (Philippians 4:9 ASV)

Notes

44

Ideas to Improve

Believe it or not, the boss may not always have the best ideas for everything. Your employees are pretty awesome too and may have some great ideas to share. Don't dismiss your employees' ideas, even if their ideas are not your first pick at the time. Encourage them to use their knowledge to improve upon the workplace and maybe even come up with possible changes of their own that can bring value. Things are always changing, and improvements are made every day. When we start thinking our way is the only way, we need a serious reality check.

Humble yourselves in the sight of the Lord, and he shall exalt you. (James 4:10 ASV)

Notes

45

Reaping the Rewards

Knowing you are valued is important, and everyone needs to be able to hear it once in a while. More important, however, is putting something behind those words. Actions are a bit louder than words, so reward your employees when possible. Financially, we can't hand out raises like candy, but there are other options to make them feel rewarded. I vote for chocolate! Think about implementing an affordable rewards program that works best for your workplace while still benefiting your employees.

Through him then let us offer up a sacrifice of praise to God continually, that is, the fruit of lips which make confession to his name. (Hebrews 13:15 ASV)

Notes

46

Honesty Still Beats All

Honesty is still a pretty good policy. I swear I'm not lying, but how we say the truth is an entirely different story. We tend to either sugarcoat everything to the point of no return or swing to the other side to brutal bluntness. Sure we need to be honest. It is a must in ethics. But also opt for appropriate honesty, knowing how and when to speak the truth appropriately. It's easy to speak your mind but not always the best choice. Think before you speak. You will be glad you did. Honest!

He that spareth his words hath knowledge; And he that is of a cool spirit is a man of understanding. (Proverbs 17:27 ASV)

Notes

47

Sandwich Approach

Sure, you probably have heard of the sandwich approach—two sincere compliments with a constructive correction in the middle—but is it ever used? Or do we tend to forget the bread and just focus on the meat in the middle? We always will have things to improve, correct, and critique, but also find the good in your employees' work. It wouldn't be a sandwich without those two slices of bread! Sometimes as humans, we just need to have those carbs!

Let no corrupt speech proceed out of your mouth, but such as is good for edifying as the need may be, that it may give grace to them that hear. (Ephesians 4:29 ASV)

Notes

48

Drop a Line

OK, maybe we don't actually write letters much these days, but however you do it, it still can go a long way. So next time someone does something special, or just maybe needs a little pick-me-up, let them know. If it's a call, text, email, or even a tweet, reach out and let someone know they are appreciated. I remember my boss would group text the team to thank us for a job well done on a project, and I still have a letter of congratulations from a boss years ago. It may seem trivial, but the little things really do make a big difference.

So then let us follow after things which make for peace, and things whereby we may edify one another. (Romans 14:19 ASV)

Notes

49

Correct in Private

Have you been in one of those awkward moments where you watch your colleague get chewed out by your boss and it's in front of everyone? You feel bad for your teammate but are secretly glad it wasn't you this time? Some may be thicker-skinned, but either way, it is just plain brutal (and unprofessional) to tear someone down in front of others. You may be upset and your employee may need to be counseled, but do it at the right time and in the right place: in a private setting with the appropriate people involved and your temper in check. Take note of the effectiveness and hope your boss will do the same if you ever have a turn in the hot seat.

He that is slow to anger is of great understanding; But he that is hasty of spirit exalteth folly. (Proverbs 14:29 ASV)

Notes

50

Praise in Public

Who does not love a compliment? I'll take all that I can get, especially at my age! It's human nature to want to be praised, and just like correcting, it has an effective time and place. Exploit your team accomplishments and achievements for them to see. It encourages them to continue, try even harder, and can even drive a little healthy competition when they see others are getting recognized for a job well done. You don't want any peacocks, but a little bit of accolades never hurt either.

Let each one of us please his neighbor for that which is good, unto edifying. (Romans 15:2 ASV)

Notes

51

Do What's Right, Even When No One Is Looking

This statement pretty much sums up the meaning of character. It might be easy to do what is right when you know you are on display, but how about if you know you would never get caught? When you know no one is around? I once heard we act our true selves when we are alone, and I've got to admit it holds some truth. Granted, we probably would not walk around in our underwear in public, but what about ethical choices? I once had a manager tell me about a stop sign in the middle of nowhere and the temptation was always to glide through it. Instead, he made it his mini moral test as a reminder to do what's right every day, even when we don't want to. We will always have our versions of that stop sign in life, so choose wisely.

He that walketh uprightly walketh surely; But he that perverteth his ways shall be known. (Proverbs 10:9 ASV)

Notes

52

Set the Mood

You set the harmony for the workplace and the precedent for your employees to emulate. We all remember days when word quickly spreads that the boss was in a bad mood just by how his or her demeanor was when they came through the front door. Even when we are stressed, upset, or just cranky, we shouldn't show it to our team. Moods are contagious and will quickly spread, good or bad. Ever heard of the very true statement that when the mom is happy, everyone is happy? Why? Because the mom would usually set the tone for the household to follow. No one is perfect and you can't always be expected to be on happy pills, but as a leader, you have a responsibility to your team for others to follow, so get in the mood!

Then was our mouth filled with laughter, And our tongue with singing: Then said they among the nations, Jehovah hath done great things for them. (Psalm 126:2 ASV)

Notes

53

Relationships Are a No-No

You work with your team several days a week, get to know them, and are a part of each other's life, whether you like it or not! However, while colleagues may be friends after work, it's a little different with boss and employee relationships. As a leader of your team, you cannot play favorites and your relationships must be professional. No one likes a skirt (or pants) chaser, and once you get a bad reputation, it is hard to lose it. A stellar reputation, however, is hard to come by and can be lost with just one bad choice, so treat it like the priceless commodity that it is.

A righteous man that walketh in his integrity, Blessed are his children after him. (Proverbs 20:7 ASV)

Notes

54

Don't Be Afraid to Make Mistakes

My husband is a risk-taker, and I tend to avoid risks like the plague! Any great leader didn't get to where they are by never making a mistake and always playing it safe. Sometimes you have to take calculated risks, take chances, and make mistakes. Don't focus on the errors, but learn from them or you will never move on from point A to point B. Use the mistakes you made as a tool to know how to proceed. Edison didn't give up on working on the light bulb when it didn't work at first. He simply said, "I have not failed. I've just found 10,000 ways that it won't work."

He shall not be afraid of evil tidings: His heart is fixed, trusting in Jehovah. (Psalm 112:7 ASV)

Notes

55

Don't Take Work Home

I could be the poster child for this one! I had to learn how to compartmentalize and keep myself from taking my work life home with me, and I am still working on that one. There will always be work, always things to get done, but you may not always have that special time with your loved ones. Sometimes you have to draw the line and know when to put work aside to spend time with your family, friends, and yourself. And until someone invents a time machine, you will never get those moments back, so don't squander precious time that you will later look back on and regret.

Better is a dinner of herbs, where love is, Than a stalled ox and hatred therewith. (Proverbs 15:17 ASV)

Notes

56

Don't Worry

Don't worry. Be happy. If it was only as simple as the saying goes. Everyone worries sometimes; it is part of being human. However, too much is going to wear you out and bring you down. Speaking from hard experience, worrying does not help any situation, but facing the issues that you are worried about does help resolve the matter. As a leader, being prepared, organized, and ready to handle opportunities head-on will go a long way in keeping your stress under control.

Heaviness in the heart of a man maketh it stoop; But a good word maketh it glad. (Proverbs 12:25 ASV)

Notes

57

Take a Break

Sometimes we are so focused on work we forget that our minds and bodies simply need a break. However short, we each come back more focused and rejuvenated with a refreshed spirit. Don't forget that you, as well as your employees, need them. Sure, there will be plenty of times you realized you worked straight through the lunch hour, but it should not be the norm. Take a breather and go have lunch in the park or a quick walk around the block if time permits. Escape and unwind for a few short moments before putting your nose back to the grindstone.

Go thy way, eat thy bread with joy, and drink thy wine with a merry heart; for God hath already accepted thy works. (Ecclesiastes 9:7 ASV)

Notes

58

Don't Let Titles Rule

Imagine letting your circumstances of birth dictate what you'll achieve. It may seem medieval, but history proves that humans love labels, and it is still evident today. Don't let your title become who you are, and don't let them divide you and your team. I toured a car plant years ago where everyone, from the rookie to the head supervisor, wore the same uniform, right down to the name tag. Although they had different roles and responsibilities, they were equals, leaving little room for a big man on campus mentality. It's great to be proud of the career goals you have achieved, but don't rely on your title to achieve results.

There can be neither Jew nor Greek, there can be neither bond nor free, there can be no male and female; for ye all are one man in Christ Jesus. (Galatians 3:28 ASV)

Notes

59

Five Minutes a Day Keeps HR Away

If you work for a large company or a corporation, then you are probably familiar with human resources. While HR is a fantastic tool to ensure your company is following protocol, you don't exactly relish a personal visit from them either. Try spending a few moments with each of your associates every day to see how they are doing. If you have a large number of associates, then even just a friendly greeting when making your rounds shows you care. Follow up on any possible incidents. It will not go away if you just ignore it, and facing the matter is better than hiding. Knowing what's going on in your workplace, talking to your employees, and addressing their concerns will help you put out any sparks before they burst into flames.

It is an abomination to kings to commit wickedness; For the throne is established by righteousness. Righteous lips are the delight of kings; And they love him that speaketh right. (Proverbs 16:12–13 ASV)

Notes

60

Lead by Inspiration, Not Intimidation

When you think of bosses, Mr. Rogers and Barney are probably not the first images that come to mind. More likely the Incredible Hulk or Mr. Burns from *The Simpsons.* So why as leaders do we feel that we always have to rule the land with an iron fist? Yes, it will probably get the job done just the same, but is it inspired by respect and admiration for their honorable leader or fear and loathing for the mean boss they ridicule behind closed doors? Do you want your team to follow you just because they have to or because they want to? Leading by fear may get you short-term results, but you will not see a return unless you invest into your employees the leadership they deserve.

When the righteous are increased, the people rejoice; But when a wicked man beareth rule, the people sigh. (Proverbs 29:2 ASV)

Notes

61

Affirmations for You and Your Employees

Ever do New Year's resolutions? Starting a diet, exercising every day, and my personal favorite, no more pizza! Those resolutions, for me at least, usually last a few days, maybe a week if I'm really good. I find that if I really want to make a change, then I can do it any time, whether it's January or July. Realistic affirmations are a great tool for you and your team to utilize as a group or even solo. Taking the time to write them, speak them, and revisit them is a positive reinforcement for your team to help visualize and focus on the goals they hope to achieve.

And Jehovah answered me, and said, Write the vision, and make it plain upon tablets, that he may run that readeth it. (Habakkuk 2:2 ASV)

Notes

62

You Are What You Write

Thank God for spell-check. But even that can't replace correct grammar and a basic comprehension of writing skills. While this may have been drilled into us since grade school, we tend to lose it if we don't use it! Be knowledgeable in your writing and speaking skills (or just get an app for it!), especially in the workplace. It reflects your professionalism, intelligence, and an ability to interact in an ever-changing environment.

Incline thine ear, and hear the words of the wise,
And apply thy heart unto my knowledge. (Proverbs
22:17 ASV)

Notes

63

Take Pride on and off the Clock

Even though the dictionary can make the word *proud* sound like you're pretty boastful, it also states, when used in the adjective form, that pride is self-respect, self-esteem, and honorable. Take pride in the work that you do and how you do it. There is something extremely satisfying about taking a step back and viewing a job well done. Don't just save it for when you are on the job. Even in your personal life, everything worth doing is usually worth doing well. There is moderation in everything, and no one likes a big ego, but be proud of who you are. You're worth it.

Whether therefore ye eat, or drink, or whatsoever ye do, do all to the glory of God. (1 Corinthians 10:31 ASV)

Notes

64

Roll Up Your Sleeves

It may not come up very often, but show your team that you're still willing and able to use some good old elbow grease. You probably have had a few bosses like I had, the ones who always made you feel like they were just a little too good to work with the crew. They may never even have had that thought, but their actions indicated otherwise. Years ago, I remember when we had a huge cleanup after a major storm damaged our workplace. We all showed up, ready to clean up and get dirty, and our supervisor worked side by side with us every step of the way. He wasn't afraid to roll up his sleeves, and that thought still sticks with me years later. Be the boss you want to work for.

In all things showing thyself an ensample of good works; in thy doctrine showing uncorruptness, gravity, sound speech, that cannot be condemned; that he that is of the contrary part may be ashamed, having no evil thing to say of us. (Titus 2:7–8 ASV)

Notes

65

Pass It On

Paying it forward and giving back to communities can give even the biggest scrooge the warm fuzzies. There are endless opportunities where we can give back to those in need, organizations that we can donate our time to, and facilities that desperately need financial resources to keep their doors open. Even our talents can be used to lend a helping hand. Everyone leaves an imprint on this world. Make yours a positive one. It's not how much you give; it's that you give.

Let each man do according as he hath purposed in his heart: not grudgingly, or of necessity: for God loveth a cheerful giver. (2 Corinthians 9:7 ASV)

Notes

66

Are You Listening to Me, Dear?

I have a habit, like many wives, to ramble a little bit to my husband. I sometimes get the feeling he may not be hanging on my every word about the cute dress and shoes I bought today. Can you imagine? At least his hearing improves when I tell him how much I spent! Seriously, take time to really listen to your employees; their input and thoughts are important. Don't be quick to do all the talking or just thinking about what you are going to say next. Most people love to hear the sound of their own voice. Just make sure your voice is not the only one being heard.

And he said unto them, Take heed what ye hear: with what measure ye mete it shall be measured unto you; and more shall be given unto you. (Mark 4:24 ASV)

Notes

67

Go the Extra Mile

If you have ever run in a race, then you know about a runner's second wind. The feeling you get when you think you are at the end of your rope but then find the energy to continue with renewed strength and stamina. Often in life, we find ourselves at a point where we feel where we can go no more and push ourselves to the very end. Then suddenly we catch our second wind and push ourselves to greatness. If we never push ourselves and go that extra mile, then we will never know what we could have achieved. As Twain once said, "Twenty years from now, you will be more disappointed by the things you didn't do than the things you did do."

Therefore let us also, seeing we are compassed about with so great a cloud of witnesses, lay aside every weight, and the sin which doth so easily beset us, and let us run with patience the race that is set before us. (Hebrews 12:1 ASV)

Notes

68

No Doubt about It

By nature, I am a complete realist. While it may be a good quality at times, don't let your mind get in the way of your heart. Too often we put limits on our own success with no one to blame but ourselves. We start doubting ourselves and question the talents we have been gifted. While we still have to deal with reality and the here and now, we can't question the seeds deep inside that sprout into the dreams that make us unique.

For we are his workmanship, created in Christ Jesus for good works, which God afore prepared that we should walk in them. (Ephesians 2:10 ASV)

Notes

69

Just Imagine

My husband is quite a visionary, always thinking about the possibilities. I often envy him at times, as I have my feet firmly planted on the ground. More like cemented! But just think of how our world could be if we just used a little bit more of our imagination. All of us are born with an imagination, and it is usually widely used during our childhood years. As we grow into young adults, we start putting away childish things and tend to include our imagination into that category. While as adult leaders we may no longer have an imaginary friend, we also don't want to squander the imagination deep inside each of us. So dream on!

I can do all things in him that strengtheneth me.
(Philippians 4:13 ASV)

Notes

70

Don't Be a Thermostat

Tempers can flare and people can quickly go from hot to cold. Self-control is a sign of maturity, and we must learn to stay calm and levelheaded. Don't be a hothead or—even worse—regret something you did or said rashly. We are going to get mad, upset, and want to tear out our hair, maybe even someone else's hair! As leaders, we must keep our emotions under control and in check. We would live in a world of total chaos if we gave into our impulses, so don't let your emotions rule the roost.

Cease from anger, and forsake wrath: Fret not thyself, it tendeth only to evil-doing. (Psalm 37:8 ASV)

Notes

71

Employees? Associates?

Employees are generally termed as people who work for you, and associates are defined as people who work with you and own a piece of the pie. I had once worked for a great company that always frowned upon calling those they employed employees; they were termed associates. While it is a nice touch for those you employ to be considered associates, it is essentially considered the same thing unless you differentiate it with ownership. If you are going to have associates instead of employees, then stand behind it with meaning and benefits to substantiate the difference. A feeling of belonging is a powerful thing, but back it up with more than just fancy euphuism.

We therefore ought to welcome such, that we may be fellow-workers for the truth. (3 John 1:8 ASV)

Notes

72

We Are Family

Smaller companies usually have the luxury of a close-knit, family-like atmosphere. Larger corporations tend to lose this edge and often struggle with red tape getting in the way. Politics, lawyers, and policies are musts to protect your assets, but they can also replace the small-town feel that may have once existed. Just as in relationships, keeping families together takes work, dedication, and nurturing. Just because your company has grown does not mean you have to lose the family atmosphere. The same rules apply, just on a larger scale. Make a conscious decision to invest the time and effort needed to make your workplace the setting for a family to grow.

And above all these things put on love, which is the bond of perfectness. (Colossians 3:14 ASV)

Notes

73

123, Huddle

You see it all the time on a football field, the quick huddles to discuss the next strategic move for a goal. It is just as essential in the work field to have daily huddles for your team to gather and confer. Just as you see in sports, it does not have to be long-winded but is simply a quick regroup to ensure you are on the same play. While the quarterback or team captain usually leads the huddle, it is also a time for your team to share their ideas as well. Make the time to have one every day you work, and help lead your team to victory.

Let your speech be always with grace, seasoned with salt, that ye may know how ye ought to answer each one. (Colossians 4:6 ASV)

Notes

74

Going through the Motions

Do you ever have one of those days where you just go through the motions? Where you are so preoccupied you feel like your body is on autopilot? You can drive to work and don't even remember getting there. Been there too. But life should not be lived out in that realm. We have employees who do the same. They do a decent job but never really reach their potential; their hearts are not really in it. They never make a commitment to be part of the team, just driving by in life and never noticing the scenery. Have only team players on your team, not players who happen to be on your team, as there is a difference. For you and your team to reach your full potential, work to ensure you are not just getting by. Life is too short and there is still a road ahead, so enjoy the view.

Know ye not that they that run in a race run all, but one receiveth the prize? Even so run; that ye may attain. (1 Corinthians 9:24 ASV)

Notes

75

Icebreakers

The awkward silence when you can hear a pin drop, someone coughs, a chair screeches. You're in one of those meetings where no one is really comfortable. If your meetings with your team are just plain awkward or you have some new members, then take the strides to make your entire team comfortable. If they are in a relaxed environment, they are more likely to be open, attentive, and sharing ideas. Icebreakers are a great avenue to make that happen; consider teams or groups for them as some may not enjoy having the spotlight. They can be about anything but should always be appropriate, fun, and inviting.

And as ye would that men should do to you, do ye also to them likewise. (Luke 6:31 ASV)

Notes

76

Don't Just Comply

Do you ever feel like there is a report for everything? While your tasks may include a lot of paperwork, remember there is someone who probably needs those figures or facts and is vital to your workplace on some level. Just about every realm of business has to comply with regulations, laws, and rules. Don't forget that while the work can be tedious, it is part of a bigger picture for which everyone has an essential role.

Consider what I say; for the Lord shall give thee understanding in all things. (2 Timothy 2:7 ASV)

Notes

77

Make Meetings Fun?

"Bueller, Bueller." Imagine if you had the teacher from the Ferris Bueller movie leading your meetings! OK, so your meetings are not that bad, but they could probably be a little more stimulating. Don't want anyone drooling on the tables after falling asleep! Obviously, you have meetings for a reason and a need to communicate important information to your employees. How you do it is another story. Make them fun while still being productive. While you are including your results and goals, don't forget about recognition and praise. End your meetings on a positive note, and while you may have to talk about the bad, always include the good.

Rejoicing in hope; patient in tribulation; continuing stedfastly in prayer. (Romans 12:12 ASV)

Notes

78

For Better or for Worse

No, I'm not actually talking about marriage; a career can be just as big of a commitment. Your workplace will be better or worse because of you, and the level of commitment you decide to invest is completely up to you. Don't get cold feet. Decide to make a vow of commitment today so that years from now you will be able to look back, hold your head high, and know that you made your company better, even if just a little.

Let your heart therefore be perfect with Jehovah our God, to walk in his statutes, and to keep his commandments, as at this day. (1 Kings 8:61 ASV)

Notes

79

Watch Your Tongue

When we were visiting Virginia Beach, they once had signs reminding tourists to watch what they say, to apparently keep the public area family oriented. Biting your tongue, having a money jar, or—yikes—having your kids repeat what you said may help you kick the habit. Regardless, it is never the picture of professionalism to be known as the one with the foul mouth. As a leader, you are setting the example, so keep the loose lips in check. Think about what you are saying and if your words are building people up or tearing people down.

But now do ye also put them all away: anger, wrath, malice, railing, shameful speaking out of your mouth. (Colossians 3:8 ASV)

Notes

80

Don't Panic

Take a deep breath into that paper bag; it is not the end of the world. You are the captain, and if you start panicking, then your ship will be sinking fast. Keep your cool even if you don't feel it. Remember that deodorant commercial from years ago? "Soft & Dri will help hide when you're feeling nervous inside." It's OK to be nervous, even scared, when something does not according to plan, but how you perform under pressure will prepare you to weather those storms in the future.

Be not therefore anxious for the morrow: for the morrow will be anxious for itself. Sufficient unto the day is the evil thereof. (Matthew 6:34 ASV)

Notes

81

Cross-Training

In the workforce, it is sometimes financially impossible to cross-train your employees. However, if you have the resources, take the time to have your employees train with each other so they can fill in as necessary. We tend to procrastinate, thinking we will have time later. But when someone is out sick or on vacation, then you will be wishing that you did. It's great to be optimistic, but be prepared like a pessimist.

Every prudent man worketh with knowledge; But a fool flaunteth his folly. (Proverbs 13:16 ASV)

Notes

82

Back to the Basics

Technology and gadgets are a lifesaver in the hustle and bustle of today's busy world, but sometimes you just need to unplug. I keep my phone on me twenty-four/seven. I look at it almost compulsively and sometimes don't even know why. My husband, daughter, and I went out to dinner the other day, and I noticed that although we were together, we were on our phones, doing our own things. As a leader, you will also be immersed in technology; it is a part of our world. Just don't forget to step back every so often. You'll be more focused and less stressed for it and enjoy the simpler things in life.

Come unto me, all ye that labor and are heavy laden, and I will give you rest. (Matthew 11:28 ASV)

Notes

83

Follow-Up on Follow-Through

Do you ever ask your employees to do something and never follow up to see if it is done? You ask them if they got it done. "Oh yes, it's finished, just like you asked." But their version and your version of follow-through may be on two completely different planets. As a leader, you are ultimately responsible for your team's work, so inspect certain tasks you delegate. Take time to follow up on follow-through, and avoid looking like a fool.

The wise shall inherit glory; But shame shall be the promotion of fools. (Proverbs 3:35 ASV)

Notes

84

Understand Strengths and Weaknesses

Believe it or not, we actually have weaknesses as well as strengths. More importantly, we need to embrace our strengths while we are improving our weaknesses. You also need to get to know your employees to find out what they are good at. Once you do, then place your team where their talents will be most valuable. This doesn't mean that we give up on our weaknesses but continue to work on them while continuing to improve our strengths. I love to sing in the car, but all the work in the world will probably never make me the next great superstar; however, that doesn't mean that I will stop singing, even if my voice can probably attract the neighborhood dogs.

But let each man prove his own work, and then shall he have his glorying in regard of himself alone, and not of his neighbor. (Galatians 6:4 ASV)

Notes

85

Organization

I remember when my teams used to call me OCD because I had our workplace so organized. It may have bordered on the unhealthy side, but it certainly kept everything organized, orderly, and easy to find. Everything has a place, so take the measures to get things organized. Once you do, then make sure that it stays that way, which can be half the battle. If you don't have that orderly gene, then assign it to one of your employees who does and get your entire team on the same page. If you don't support something, then no one else will either, so get your ducks in a row.

And when he is come, he findeth it swept and garnished. (Luke 11:25 ASV)

Notes

86

Preparation

If you ever watched one of those prepper shows, then you know they are ready for just about anything. While I'm not suggesting to build a bunker, you still have to be prepared for what comes your way. Being prepared is part of being a good leader. While your workplace may not be as intense as a doomsdayer's, still take measures to be ready for the unexpected. Any good business will encounter challenges, and how you prepare for them will determine the success of you, your team, and your company.

A prudent man seeth the evil, and hideth himself;
But the simple pass on, and suffer for it. (Proverbs
22:3 ASV)

Notes

87

Remember Where You Came From

We are all equals, and although we come from different backgrounds and cultures, we all come from the same place. Remember the days when you were in those rookie shoes and how it felt to wear them? Even though you may now have achieved greatness, don't forget that we are in this together and the title doesn't make the person. Remember where you came from, and occasionally eat a slice of that humble pie.

I charge thee in the sight of God, and Christ Jesus, and the elect angels, that thou observe these things without prejudice, doing nothing by partiality. (1 Timothy 5:21 ASV)

Notes

88

An Eagle or a Duck?

My husband once heard the analogy to be an eagle, not a duck, and I always had a hard time relating as I think ducks are super cute. However, the analogy has some definite merit. Look at eagles and how they soar. They don't go with the norm but choose to soar above in everything they do. Ducks, however, often quack and complain, waddling around and never doing much more than that. Don't just settle for ordinary. Soar for success, and make it extraordinary.

But they that wait for Jehovah shall renew their strength; they shall mount up with wings as eagles; they shall run, and not be weary; they shall walk, and not faint. (Isaiah 40:31 ASV)

Notes

89

No Walls

Remember as children when we would pitch a fit and take all of our toys home if we had a fight with our friends? Now as adults, we may no longer gather our toys and go crying to Mom, but we still find ourselves putting up walls. We divide ourselves from other departments, even in our own company, simply out of selfishness, fear, or a "me" mentality. We have to be willing to work together with those on the same team. This doesn't mean being walked on, but it does mean to consider how much you can accomplish when you come together.

For the body is not one member, but many. (1 Corinthians 12:14 ASV)

Notes

90

Smile for the Camera

I remember watching an old episode of *The Brady Bunch* where Alice had written an old family recipe on the chalkboard that accidentally got erased, much to her chagrin. But wait. Greg had inadvertently taken a picture of it and the day was saved! How many times in real life did we wish we took a picture of how things looked at near perfection? We take pictures of weight loss, family moments, and countless other memories. Consider taking pictures in the workforce as well, to ensure that what is supposed to be is actually reality. It is a great training tool when your employees are being developed and is a good reminder for yourself as well. While you may not be an Ansel Adams, your pictures could be worth a lot more than just a thousand words.

I remember the days of old; I meditate on all thy doings; I muse on the work of thy hands. (Psalm 143:5 ASV)

Notes

91

Squeaky Clean

No one likes a slob. Even if you are the nicest guy in the world, being dirty is just plain gross. My husband used to be called "Mr. White Glove" because he expected high standards of sanitation. Ever see those dirty restrooms that make you want to hold it? Or the dirty counter and the filthy preparing areas you get a peek of? It really does matter, and your customers are going to notice. If you don't notice these types of things, look at your business objectively and then train yourself and your team to raise your standards of cleanliness. Now go get those proverbial white gloves and get busy!

Jesus, knowing that the Father had given all things into his hands, and that he came forth from God, and goeth unto God. (John 13:3 ASV)

Notes

92

Tug-of-War

It's a fierce competition in this dog-eat-dog world and you will always have competition for your customers and their business. Never fear though as good, healthy competition keeps everyone on their toes. Having to compete may mean you and your team have to work harder, but you will reap the rewards if you continue to push through and never give up on improving. Know who your competitors are, and be willing to admit if they are better than you. Just as in battle, you may have to retreat and rework your strategy. Never give up, and continue to soldier on.

Have not I commanded thee? Be strong and of good courage; be not affrighted, neither be thou dismayed: for Jehovah thy God is with thee whithersoever thou goest. (Joshua 1:9 ASV)

Notes

93

A Breath of Fresh Air

Going outside and getting some air usually makes everyone feel a little bit better. I don't know whether it is the natural vitamin D or it's just psychological, but either way, it's refreshing to have a renewed outlook. In the workplace, sometimes we need some fresh air breathed into our environment; we become stagnant and set in our old ways. Things change, positions change, and companies adapt to keep up with the ever-changing needs to satisfy the customer. However, humans are not always good at this thing called change. It may be a bitter pill to swallow, but as a leader, we sometimes have to consider the needs of the company before ourselves and be willing to adapt for a better tomorrow.

Remember ye not the former things, neither consider the things of old. (Isaiah 43:18 ASV)

Notes

94

Reuse to Recycle

I'm often called a tree hugger by my family and friends. I have to admit I truly love the earth and all the cute, furry friends that live on it. While it may be no big deal to never think twice of throwing a bunch of papers away, take a moment to consider if everyone had that same mentality. Think of our future leaders, not to mention the financial benefits of recycling, even if it is just in your employees' lounge. Even if you don't personally agree with recycling, as a leader, take a stance to support it and go a little green.

And Jehovah God took the man, and put him into the garden of Eden to dress it and to keep it. (Genesis 2:15 ASV)

Notes

95

Congrats! You Got the Job!

What exciting words to give someone. Just make sure it's the right someone. If it is time for you to hire, always do it for the right reasons, at the right time, and with the right people. Don't rush into hiring the first person to walk in just because you need someone immediately to relieve the workload. Doing so will just make it worse and give you something else to worry about. Be thorough in your interviews, regardless of whether you are interviewing for a supervisor or a busboy. Taking extra time in an interview may mean the difference between having to deal later with a superstar or a nightmare.

A false balance is an abomination to Jehovah; But a just weight is his delight. (Proverbs 11:1 ASV)

Notes

96

Crystal Ball

Let me take a closer look into my crystal ball to see your future. If only it were so silly or simple. While we may not be able to see our future, we can certainly prepare for it. Have a business plan in place for your company, even if it is just a plan for your personal career goals. Your company and your career will likely be different five and ten years from now than they are today; you will grow, learn, and be better for it. Make plans today to achieve what you want to accomplish in the future, and leave the palm reading to those fortune tellers.

For I know the thoughts that I think toward you, saith Jehovah, thoughts of peace, and not of evil, to give you hope in your latter end. (Jeremiah 29:11 ASV)

Notes

97

One of a Kind

Too often in the business world, we mask our individuality to blend in with the rest of society. We hide our creativity in fear of being different and conceal our uniqueness that was created to shine. Don't hide your light under a bushel! While we may have to be in uniforms, consistent with regulations, and comply with laws, it does not mean we have to be something that we are not. As far I know, humans are not created on an assembly line in a mass-producing factory plant. Celebrate the wonderful person that you are, and encourage others to do the same!

I will give thanks unto thee; for I am fearfully and wonderfully made: Wonderful are thy works; And that my soul knoweth right well. (Psalm 139:14 ASV)

Notes

98

A Walk in Another's Shoes

It's easy and natural to get caught up in our troubles. We are a busy society that is sometimes too busy to think much about others outside our plastic bubble. While you don't want to be the local therapist, what about those we interact with every day? Take a minute, think of your team, and put yourself in their place sometimes. While you can't let their problems overrun yours, you can let them know that as their leader you care.

And the King shall answer and say unto them,
Verily I say unto you, Inasmuch as ye did it unto
one of these my brethren, even these least, ye did it
unto me. (Matthew 25:40 ASV)

Notes

99

The Food Chain

In the business world, there is a proverbial term about where we are on the food chain. Hate to break it to you, but while it may feel like a jungle out there, we are not actually tigers and bears. Although we may act like beasts sometimes, humans are equals and should be treated as such. You have a world full of reports, emails, and demands to keep you going. Just don't get so tied up in trying to climb the corporate ladder that you forget that people are the priority.

Forget not to show love unto strangers: for thereby
some have entertained angels unawares. (Hebrews
13:2 ASV)

Notes

100

Is Your Heart Really in It?

Are you passionate about what you do? For the most part, do you love it? Do you enjoy your career? Or do you do it just because it pays the bills? Do you always dread going to work? I'm not talking about Monday morning blues but sick-to-your-stomach dread. If it sounds like I have been there, it is because I have. I had been at a point where my job made me physically sick and the only way I got through is counting the minutes until the end of my shift or my next day off. That isn't how it should be! I do not have a magical lamp to answer this dilemma, but I can tell you from experience that while it may be sometimes necessary to stay in a job for financial reasons, etc., don't make that a permanent place! I hope you're never there, I hope you love your job, but if you don't and you are there, make plans to move toward your heart's desire. If you don't know what that is, then find it!

For where thy treasure is, there will thy heart be also. (Matthew 6:21 ASV)

Notes

Work Cited

Barney & Friends. Directed by Fred Holmes. Performed by Bob West, Julie Johnson. Lyons Group, 1992. VHS.

The Brady Bunch. Directed by Sherwood Schwartz. Performed by Robert Reed, Florence Henderson. Paramount Home Entertainment, 2005. DVD.

Ferris Bueller's Day Off. Directed by John Hughes. Performed by Matthew Broderick, Alan Ruck, Mia Sara. Paramount Home Entertainment, 2006. DVD.

The Incredible Hulk. Directed by Bill Bixby. Performed by Bill Bixby, Lou Ferrigno. Universal Studios Home Entertainment, 2008. DVD.

The Little Mermaid. Written by H. C. Andersen. Performed by Jodi Benson. StarMaker Entertainment, 1989. DVD.

Lurker, Internet. "Soft & Dri Deodorant Commercial with Jingle." YouTube, September 30, 2010. September 18, 2014.

Mister Rogers' Neighborhood. Directed by Fred Rogers. Performed by Fred Rogers. Anchor Bay Entertainment, 2005. VHS.

The Simpsons. Directed by Matt Groening. Performed by Dan Castellaneta, Nancy Cartwright. 20th Century Fox Home Entertainment, 2005. DVD.

Holy Bible: American Standard Version.

Printed in the United States
by Baker & Taylor Publisher Services